There Is Only One Thing Worse Than Going to Hell

And How to Avoid It!

DAVID JUWEL

WORD & SPIRIT
PUBLISHING

This report is designed to provide accurate and authoritative information regarding the subject matter covered. It is professional advice based on divine authority and Spirit-led illumination.

Unless otherwise indicated, all Scriptures quoted are from the King James Version of the Bible.

Scripture quotations marked AMP are taken from the Amplified® Bible (AMP), Copyright © 2015 by The Lockman Foundation. Used by permission. www.lockman.org.

Scripture quotations marked ESV are taken from the ESV® Bible (The Holy Bible, English Standard Version®), copyright © 2001 by Crossway Bibles, a publishing ministry of Good News Publishers. ©All rights reserved.

Any **bold** print in Scripture references has been added by the author for emphasis. The **emboldened** print is not part of the original translation.

There Is Only One Thing Worse Than Going to Hell And How to Avoid It!
Copyright © 2025 by David Juwel
ISBN: 978-1-685730-71-0

Published by Word and Spirit Publishing
P.O. Box 701403
Tulsa, Oklahoma 74170
wordandspiritpublishing.com

Printed in the United States of America. All rights reserved under International Copyright Law. Content and/or cover may not be reproduced in whole or in part in any form without the expressed written consent of the Publisher.

Contents

Introduction v

Here's the Problem 1

Further Reasons Why This Problem Exists 15

Are All the Preceding Statements Simply
Religious Arrogance? 21

Sincerity Is Not the Key to Spiritual Well-Being 29

How Can I Tell If Am a Mature Christian? 31

What Can I Do to Make Sure I Am Maturing in the Lord? 43

Here Is Another Checklist to Follow 47

Benediction 49

About the Author 51

Introduction

MY MOTIVE FOR WRITING THIS book is found in the following Scriptures:

How then shall they call on him in whom they have not believed? and how shall they believe in him of whom they have not heard? and how shall they hear without a preacher?

—Romans 10:14

Let him know, that he which converteth the sinner from the error of his way shall save a soul from death, and shall hide a multitude of sins.

—James 5:20

And the very God of peace sanctify you wholly; and I pray God your whole spirit and soul and body be preserved blameless unto the coming of our Lord Jesus Christ.

—1 Thessalonians 5:23

I pray that your heart, soul, and mind will be so infused with the truth that it will inspire you to become a bona-fide living and *obedient* servant of the King of kings and Lord of lords, Jesus Christ.

Here's the Problem

THERE IS ONLY ONE THING worse than going to hell, and that is . . .

Going to Hell While Sincerely Believing That You Are Going to Heaven

One of the greatest tragedies about the preceding fact is that there are a great many church members who are in this predicament. The problem is that they are not aware of it.

In fact, a very prominent church leader once said that perhaps only 30 percent of the people in all our churches are bona-fide Christians, even though 100 percent of them profess to be so. I believe that number is even lower today.

To help you understand why this may be such a problem, let's take a look at three specific groups of people identified in the New Testament. All three of these groups can be found in and around the church today.

The first group is identified as "**wheat.**" The word *wheat* in the New Testament refers to people who have turned their lives over to Jesus Christ. These are the people who have agreed to serve Him for the rest of their days. They represent the pure grain. They are the true children of God. Jesus calls them the children of the Kingdom.

Notice the end result of the wheat in the following Scripture:

> *Let both grow together until the harvest: and in the time of harvest I will say to the reapers, Gather ye together first the tares, and bind them in bundles to burn them: but gather the wheat into my barn.*
>
> —Matthew 13:30

The second group is identified as "**chaff.**" *Chaff* is a completely worthless seed covering that separates from the seed when the grain is threshed. Chaff is easily blown about by every change of the wind. The word *chaff* in the New Testament means that the outer layer has been beaten away from the seed inside; it is straw that has been broken. Today, I believe this could represent people who are immature in following the Lord because the enemy has succeeded in

Here's the Problem

diminishing their spiritual growth. These people have allowed the enemy to alter their spiritual growth by involving them in the cares of the world and the deceitfulness of riches, which chokes the Word.

Warning! In the "Parable of the sower," there is a comment describing someone who is living immaturely as "chaff".

> *As for what was sown on rocky ground, this is the one who hears the word and immediately receives it with joy, ^{21} yet he has no root in himself, but endures for a while, and when tribulation or persecution arises on account of the word, immediately he falls away. ^{22} As for what was sown among thorns, this is the one who hears the word, but the cares of the world and the deceitfulness of riches choke the word, and it proves unfruitful.* —Matthew 13:20-22 ESV. Cf: Psalm 1:1-4; Matthew 3:12.

You need to **diligently** continue to mature and endure in your faith to the end of your life. Don't let the chaff in the preceding scriptures describe the end of your life.

In some instances, this is a choice that occurs subtly. But the advantage they have is that they know they are spiritually immature, and they can change their minds and lives at any time by purposely drawing closer to Jesus Christ. They're just subtly backsliding, which they can resolve if they choose.

There Is Only One Thing Worse Than Going to Hell

He also that received seed among the thorns is he that heareth the word; and the care of this world, and the deceitfulness of riches, choke the word, and he becometh unfruitful. 23 But he that received seed into the good ground is he that heareth the word, and understandeth it; which also beareth fruit, and bringeth forth, some an hundredfold, some sixty, some thirty.

—Matthew 13:32,33

Notice the end result of the chaff in the following Scripture. This is what will happen if they don't diligently submit and become a true servant of the Lord before the end of their lives.

. . . and he will thoroughly purge his floor, and gather his wheat into the garner; but he will burn up the chaff with unquenchable fire.

—Matthew 3:12

Finally, the third group is identified as "**tares**." A *tare* is a false grain that can poison the true grain. Jesus calls the tares "the children of the wicked one." Jesus says the enemy that planted them is the devil. Unfortunately, this refers to people who are hypocritically fooling themselves. The problem with them is that they are deceived. They enjoy being a church member because it gives them social prestige without any responsibility. Because they are deceived, they really believe

Here's the Problem

they are a "true wheat." Consequently, they make no effort to change their way of life. The end result of their lives is the greatest tragedy that can occur to an individual, because they end up going to hell while **sincerely** believing that they are going to heaven.

The worst part of this issue is that tares also cause the modern-day church system to operate unequally yoked—that is, true Christians are joined with false believers. The Scripture has a lot to say about being unequally yoked. But we are commanded not to prune the garden lest we erroneously accuse a true Christian.

The pastor-teacher preaches and teaches his heart out, trying to get them saved. It's impossible, because in their deception, they believe they're already saved. But they can't be saved because they're children of the devil, and not of the elect. However, they can do anything in the church that doesn't require being indwelled and guided by the Holy Spirit. That willingness to falsely portray the character of a true Christian in the church camouflages their hypocrisy.

Every local church has a mixture of people who represent the wheat (true Christians), the chaff (immature people), and the tares (pseudo-Christians), filtering back and forth through it.

But there is an even greater problem with those people who are tares. As I have already stated:

They Don't Believe They Are Tares!

These people are not concerned about their actions and attitudes because they sincerely believe their actions and attitudes are normal and proper. But tares *can't* improve. They can't improve because they are not true Christians. They are not truly saved. The only thing they can do is become more religious.

People don't realize when they are "tares" because they live under a cloud of satanic deception! Satan has them believing they are "wheat" because of the religious works they can accomplish. They attend church, and they tithe. They sing the same worship songs, speak the same church language, do evangelism, teach Sunday school, and perform many other religious works. When they are in church, you can't tell the difference between them and the wheat because they act like a mirror image of the wheat. And they have absolutely no suspicion that they themselves are a tare. They sincerely believe themselves to be as saved as anyone else. They sincerely believe themselves to be a genuine Christian.

But they are simply fooling themselves, and a severe tragedy awaits them! When they die, instead of going to heaven, as they sincerely expect to do, they shall go before the Judgement Seat of God, and then be cast into the lake of fire, and there shall be wailing and gnashing of teeth. Talk about culture shock! Can you imagine what that will be like—sincerely expecting and believing that you are heaven-bound

Here's the Problem

. . . but ending up in hell for all eternity! Can you imagine the devastating irony of being involved in church life for so many years, yet ending up in hell?!

Now, the following is especially important, because I don't want to discourage you or create confusion in your life if you're a true Christian. After reading what I've just written, you may wonder whether you are a tare or not.

A "carnal Christian" can also be a true Christian who has "slipped" in a couple of areas. A carnal Christian is nothing more than basically a baby Christian. But babies quickly grow up! In fact, a person shouldn't be a "carnal Christian" for more than a year or so, because they should have become spiritually mature by that point.

However, many of these people are not growing up at all! In fact, some people have lived like this for thirty years or more. They are so secure in their self-deception that it never dawns on them how long they have lived this way. God forbid if this describes your life, because a person who lives in "perpetual carnality" is basically not a true Christian at all!

I have decided to present this problem to you, so that you can compare your life with the truth. I will provide good counsel based on the Word of God. Then it is up to you to make the needed changes in your life if the Holy Spirit convicts you of the fact that change needs to occur.

Now, before I get into the meat of this subject, I want to make something very clear. The tares are going to respond to this book by saying that you only have to *believe* in Jesus Christ to be saved. They believe that the following Scripture is the *whole* of the salvation plan:

> *That if thou shalt confess with thy mouth the Lord Jesus, and shalt believe in thine heart that God hath raised him from the dead, thou shalt be saved.*
>
> —Romans 10:9

That Scripture is true, but it contains only partial knowledge. And we often misinterpret the word *believe* in this verse. There is more to salvation than just what that scripture says. That's why God had the apostles write the twenty-one epistles, **after** the four gospels.

Many people forget that the book of Romans also contains the following verse:

> *Know ye not, that to whom ye yield yourselves servants to obey, his servants ye are to whom ye **obey**; whether of sin unto death, or of obedience unto righteousness?*
>
> —Romans 6:16

What many people don't understand is the biblical definition of the word *believe*. Today, our contemporary

Here's the Problem

understanding of the word *believe* is "mental assent" which is the acknowledgment of some fact. But the biblical definition of the word *believe* entails far more than that. It means that a divinization must occur. That simply means that Jesus came here to live like a human so that humans could learn how to live like Him. Are you?

To more clearly understand the Parable of the Seed, read Matthew 13:31-43. If you honestly compare yourself to it, you'll either be filled with joy, or you'll be fearful for your eternity. The latter may be what you need to learn.

Second Thessalonians 1:8 does not say, *"and that **believe not** the Gospel,"* nor does it say, *"and that **don't agree** with the Gospel."* It talks about those who **"don't obey"** the Gospel! The word *obey* in that Scripture is *hypakouō* in the Greek, and it means "to harken to a command, to obey, to be obedient to, or submit to." The word "Gospel" in that verse is the word *euaggelion* in the Greek, and it refers to the fact that "everything Christ did and taught" is the Good News for mankind that needs to be applied in your own life.

> *In flaming fire taking vengeance on them that know not God, and that **obey not** the gospel of our Lord Jesus Christ . . .*
>
> —2 Thessalonians 1:8

The book of Hebrews backs this up:

*And being made perfect, he became the author of eternal salvation unto all them that **obey him**.*

—Hebrews 5:9

Now, as you've read in these many Scriptures, if you don't submit your life to Jesus Christ as His servant, to *honor and obey Him*, you'll burn in the lake of Fire. It's your choice. Obey Him or don't obey Him.

Obedience is an actionable necessity, not just a mental activity.

*And why call ye me, Lord, Lord, and **do not** the things which I say?*

—Luke 6:46

Salvation requires faith and submission to Jesus Christ. The proof of your faith and submission is a lifestyle of obedience to Jesus Christ. That's why the Scriptures put so much emphasis on "works" (obedience). Works don't save you! But works are the **proof** of your commitment to Jesus Christ.

Yea, a man may say, Thou hast faith, and I have works: shew me thy faith without thy works, and I will shew thee my faith by my works. Thou believest that there is one God; thou doest well: the devils also believe, and

Here's the Problem

tremble. But wilt thou know, O vain man, that faith without works is dead? Was not Abraham our father justified by works, when he had offered Isaac his son upon the altar? Seest thou how faith wrought with his works, and by works was faith made perfect? And the scripture was fulfilled which saith, Abraham believed God, and it was imputed unto him for righteousness: and he was called the Friend of God. Ye see then how that by works a man is justified, and not by faith only. Likewise also was not Rahab the harlot justified by works, when she had received the messengers, and had sent them out another way? For as the body without the spirit is dead, so faith without works is dead also.

—James 2:18–26

I like how the Amplified Bible translates verse 26:

For just as the [human] body without the spirit is dead, so faith without works [of obedience] is also dead.

—James 2:26 AMP

You *prove* your faith in Jesus Christ by living a life of obedience to Him. That's the meaning of "works."

No obedience means no real faith. That's the difference between a true Christian and a Tare.

Now, let's look at chapter 7 of the book of Matthew, and read what the Lord said will happen to some very unsuspecting people:

Not every one that saith unto me, Lord, Lord, shall enter into the kingdom of heaven; but he that doeth the will of my Father which is in heaven. Many will say to me in that day, Lord, Lord, have we not prophesied in thy name? and in thy name have cast out devils? and in thy name done many wonderful works? And then will I profess unto them, I never knew you: depart from me, ye that work iniquity.

—Matthew 7:21–23

The Lord didn't know them because they didn't live a life of obedience to Him. They just performed religious works. Jesus said that He only did what He saw the Father doing. Shouldn't we only do what Jesus exemplified by serving and obeying the Father as Jesus did?

What a shock it will be to those people to discover that all their efforts were nothing more than wood, hay, and stubble, just worthless effort! It is obvious that they won't have any suspicion about their predicament whatsoever. These people will sincerely believe themselves to be righteous. And when they are confronted with the truth, they will try to reason with the Lord out of their sincere belief. But it

Here's the Problem

will be too late for them to do anything about it! They didn't realize that sincerity works in both ways, for righteousness and for unrighteousness.

That is why I have written this application study. Because some of your friends and neighbors may be in this predicament. Members of your own family may be in this predicament. *You* may be in this predicament!

The problem is, if you are, you won't know about it, suspect it, or even want to believe it! Someone needs to enlighten you.

Iron sharpeneth iron; so a man sharpeneth the countenance of his friend.

—Proverbs 27:17

Even as you read this study, you are probably thinking about other people, certain this study does not apply to you. And that is exactly the problem. Being saved by a shallow incomplete gospel leaves you genuinely feeling saved and needing nothing more. After all, if a simple prayer is all that's needed to save you, guaranteeing that you're heaven-bound, why do you really need to do anything more? Why not just relax and enjoy life anyway you want to (God forbid!).

However, if you are reading this study, that means it is not too late to make sure of your standing before the Lord. This study was written to help you see the difference between the wheat, the chaff, and a tare. You need to be able to look at your life and see exactly where you are in your relationship with the Lord. The information in this study will show you what you need to do to make sure you are a genuine Christian, and not a piece of chaff or a tare.

Don't let the silent epitaph over your grave proclaim:

"Here lies (your name), victim of the worst tragedy in humanity. This person went to hell while sincerely believing they were heaven-bound."

As we continue on in this study, may the grace of our Lord be upon you. May He have mercy on you. May the scales be removed from your eyes, the wax from your ears, and the hardness from your heart, so you can see, hear, and clearly understand. May the truths contained herein take root in your life for the glory of our Lord and the sake of your eternal future. Amen.

Further Reasons Why This Problem Exists

I HAVE BEEN TOLD THAT the United States is third on the list of nations where missionaries are sent. It isn't that the United States is desperately in need of evangelism. We are the most evangelized nation on the earth. The problem is that we are under-spiritualized. We are a nation that is becoming more and more "Christian," but less and less moral. We have allowed prayer to be taken out of our schools, and contrary to Scripture, physical discipline has been removed from the home, and our family unity and integrity is easily dispersed or dispensed with. Divorce is rampant, and abortion has reached epidemic levels. We are becoming more and more lawless because of our propensity for greed and our rebellion against authority of any nature. We are striving so hard to protect our freedoms that we have allowed our "wrongs" to become our "rights."

> *Withhold not correction from the child: for if thou beatest him with the rod, he shall not die. Thou shalt beat him with the rod, and shalt deliver his soul from hell.*
>
> —Proverbs 23:13–14

Part of the reason this is occurring is because of the constantly decaying spiritual nature of Christians nationwide. We (speaking for the true Christians) are the ones who are supposed to stand in the gap for other people. We are the living life savers that God has deployed throughout the earth. But you can't do it unless you learn how to swim (become discipled).

> *And I sought for a man among them, that should make up the hedge, and stand in the gap before me for the land, that I should not destroy it: but I found none.*
>
> —Ezekiel 22:30

The true Christians are supposed to be the role models. We are supposed to be the salt of leadership that helps to preserve our society. Jesus Christ is our life preserver, but we are the ones whom the Lord uses to throw that life preserver to people when they are drowning in their sins and have lost all ability or inclination to save themselves. We are supposed to be life guardians as emissaries of the Lord.

Further Reasons Why This Problem Exists

The true Christians are supposed to be spiritual leaders who are willing to swim out to those drowning and offer salvation and life preservation. And we should be willing to do this even at the risk of our own lives!

Then, once we have helped to rescue them, we are supposed to teach them how to swim, and fish, and rescue others successfully. (The Great Commission).

However, in a mistaken effort to fill our church pews, proclaim our successes, and take shortcuts for more rapid church growth, spiritual leaders around the world have watered down the presentation of the Gospel and eliminated the discipline of *applying* the Word. Now our church leaders offer people "convenience" instead of "righteousness" and entertainment instead of penetrating divine truth. Consequently, the rebuke that Jesus gave the scribes and Pharisees (the religious leaders of that day) is equally true for many of our modern-day ministers:

> *Woe unto you, scribes and Pharisees, hypocrites! for ye compass sea and land to make one proselyte, and when he is made, ye make him twofold more the child of hell than yourselves.*
>
> —Matthew 23:15

God's ministers are supposed to commit themselves exclusively to prayer, and to the ministry of the Word, while trusting wholly in the Lord for the results.

> *But we will give ourselves continually to prayer, and to the ministry of the word.*
>
> —Acts 6:4

> *Trust in the LORD with all thine heart; and lean not unto thine own understanding. In all thy ways acknowledge him, and he shall direct thy paths.*
>
> —Proverbs 3:5,6

Unfortunately, instead, too many of our church leaders are only engaged in congregational lecturing (sales), administration (management), and church growth (marketing). When that occurs, we fall into the trap of lecturing with enticing words of man's wisdom, and our sermons lack any demonstration of the Spirit or His power.

> *And my speech and my preaching was not with enticing words of man's wisdom, but in demonstration of the Spirit and of power.*
>
> —1 Corinthians 2:4

Because so **few** church leaders focus on teaching people to **apply** the Word, people have become consummate "hearers of the word" only, and they no longer exercise or discipline themselves unto godliness.

Further Reasons Why This Problem Exists

But be ye doers of the word, and not hearers only, deceiving your own selves.

—James 1:22

But refuse profane and old wives' fables, and exercise thyself rather unto godliness.

—1 Timothy 4:7

Instead, we prefer to foster and encourage an "easy believism." We do that by competing with the world in making the church entertaining, convenient, and exciting. We put on plays and musicals and have numerous outings and sporting events. We prefer superficial, worldly fellowship instead of intimate spiritual fellowship. We market the church like we would an entrepreneurial business, and very little accountability or discipline takes place.

Many of the things we do in church today do not constitute spiritual activity. They constitute religious activity. And the interesting thing about religious activity is that it can be done by both the wheat and the tares equally effective.

Helping people to commit their lives to Christ, as evidenced by the daily sacrifice of abiding obedience, is no longer the goal of the church. In order to fill the pews, it is now sufficient that people just say "yes" to Christ, and then consistently attend church, tithe, and volunteer their time and talents.

Unfortunately, the end result of all of this is that we are producing a group of people who have a form of godliness, but deny the power thereof.

Having a form of godliness, but denying the power thereof: from such turn away.

—2 Timothy 3:5

As a matter of fact, we are probably producing more tares than wheat, and we have been doing this for several decades.

Not every *body* of believers is like this. Some are true to the application of the Scriptures—but not as many as Christ would want, and that's one of the main reasons why the world scoffs at Christianity.

Are All Of the Preceding Statements Simply Religious Arrogance?

I CAN TELL YOU FROM my own personal experience that all of the statements I have made thus far represent facts gleaned from the Word of God. I was once in a sales job where I met new people in their homes on a daily basis, and because I didn't immediately reveal that I was a Christian (until an opportunity presented itself), they had a tendency to act naturally around me. Any bad habits or character they had were clearly manifested. That's because they were acting "natural," and they didn't put on a "church personality" until after they discovered that I was a Christian.

For example, one day I was meeting with a businessman in his home business. Pictures of Jesus Christ, along with crosses and other religious iconography, were strategically placed around his home. I assumed that he might be a Christian. But while we were talking, he constantly used profanity. He made several lascivious comments and was chewing tobacco, as well. His son, who was visiting, started to light up a cigarette, but the father ordered him not to do so because he didn't understand why his son had to smoke (Even though he was chewing tobacco at the time). I then used the religious articles in his house as a springboard to talk about Christianity. I asked him where he went to church. He stated that he went to the only real church in town. He then told me the name of his church (the largest one around). He said that all the other churches in town were "phony." (Does any of this sound like biblical Christianity to you?)

In addition, once we started talking about religious things, his personality changed. He stopped using profanity, started using "church language," and his attitude wasn't quite as abrasive. Imagine that.

On another occasion, I was visiting a man and his wife in their home. The television was on. While we were talking, an advertisement for a new mattress came on the TV with an attractive woman lying on the bed. He then looked at me, pointed at the television screen, and told me that he'd buy two of those beds if they'd give him two of those women to go with it. Then he burst out laughing. I didn't. I simply looked over at his wife, and when we made eye contact, she lowered her eyes and her head, ashamed and embarrassed by her husband's behavior. Later in the visit, he showed me a picture of his daughter that was hanging on the wall. He made

Are All Of the Preceding Statements Simply Religious Arrogance?

a comment about how pretty she was, and then said, "With a body like that, she can have any man she wants." I couldn't believe a father would make a comment like that about his own daughter. His comment suggested not just pride, but his approval of lascivious behavior.

At that point, I told him I was a Christian. He responded by immediately putting on a "religious hat" and using "church language." He told me he was a Christian as well, and a deacon in his church (a major denomination). Then he acted as though everything was all right. He even wanted me to "pray with him" before I left. I prayed for him instead.

One day I counseled a woman whose life was falling apart. She was failing in her health, her marriage, her employment, and in her relationship with others. She was failing in every area of her life! But every Sunday, she came to church with a Bible in one hand, and a two-inch-thick notebook in the other hand. The notebook was filled with excellent material that her pastor had taught throughout the past two years. This individual was an accomplished "hearer of the word" only. She never applied any of the biblical truths she was receiving. She sincerely believed that she was a "good Christian," and she couldn't understand why, as a "good Christian," her life was falling apart. She couldn't understand why God was allowing these things to happen to her. But it wasn't God's fault. It was happening to her because she wasn't applying any of the Christian knowledge that she had received!

I constantly meet **professing** Christians who are committing adultery, or living with a partner before marriage, or involved in illicit sexual behavior, or viewing pornography, smoking, drinking, doing drugs, lying, cheating, or stealing. Some are unable to stay employed. In many cases, they are not fellowshipping with other Christians, or they do so very infrequently. Most of these people consider themselves to be "normal" Christians, and they all sincerely think that if they died right now, they would go to heaven.

The problem is that they're really "professing, non-possessing" Christians. (What a conjunctive error that is!) The one thing all these people seem to have in common is that they all sincerely feel they can live as sinfully as they want, and act any way they want, because they've been taught that as long as they *profess* the name of Jesus, they are certain to go to heaven.

That is so completely opposite of everything expressed in Scripture! But this is a typical attitude I see over and over again among many people who call themselves "Christians." So, what's wrong with these people? Are they just simply chaff (double-minded, baby Christians)? Or are they tares?

The world, especially the news media, see people who are falling far short in their spiritual walk, and they call them "hypocrites." This has created the popular opinion that the average church is filled with **hypocrites**. I am in partial agreement with that statement. The church isn't filled with

Are All Of the Preceding Statements Simply Religious Arrogance?

hypocrites, but it has a lot of people in it who are pretending to be a Christian.

But here's the shocker: The hypocrites in the church are not true Christians at all. It's the tares who are **acting** like Christians that are sinning! They're the hypocrites! You see, a hypocrite is a person who pretends like they have a certain character or virtues that they don't really have. And that's what tares do when they attend church. They act like wheat. That is the hypocrisy the world sees! So, when the tares are away from the church, they simply revert to acting in their natural manner . . . they sin! They act exactly like what they are—unsaved Christians! Talk about a contradiction in terms. They are professing, non-possessing, "pseudo-Christians," and Jesus Christ gets the blame for their behavior because they are professing His name while they are sinning. That's what the world is seeing—tares that identify themselves as Christians—and because they identify themselves as Christians, Christianity gets a bad reputation. That is one of the reasons why Jesus *spits out* people who are neither hot nor cold.

> *So then because thou art lukewarm, and neither cold nor hot, I will **spue thee out of my mouth**.*
>
> —Revelation 3:16

When you straddle the fence, it keeps people from knowing which side you are really on. They see part of you on one side of the fence, and they don't realize that your roots are still on the other side of the fence. This problem causes people to think erroneously about the true value of Christianity.

For example, when an unsaved police officer stops a person doing 65 mph in a 45 mph zone, and that person has a Christian bumper sticker on his car, what does that officer immediately think? He thinks, *What a hypocrite this person is!*

But that's a wrong descriptor. Because they are away from the church environment, they are no longer acting like a hypocrite. They are actually acting naturally. They're a tare! They are doing whatever they want to do, just like any unsaved person does. The only problem is that they have a religious identity tag on their car, and too often that bumper sticker has the name of Jesus on it. So, Jesus gets a bad rap because another of His alleged "saints" is messing up. But the truth is, that person has no real relationship with Jesus. S/he is a phony Christian. S/he is following religion, not the Lord. And the worst part about it is that neither s/he nor the officer knows the truth!

For emphasis, let me state it again. Saying that these people are hypocrites because they act like sinners away from the church environment is an erroneous statement. The truth is, they're acting naturally then. Their hypocrisy occurs when they're in church, not outside the church! The truth is, they are actually tares. They are not saved at all.

Are All Of the Preceding Statements Simply Religious Arrogance?

Some preachers and teachers are spending an awful lot of time, talent, money, and heartache trying to help these people become mature as Christians. But it's impossible because they are not true Christians, and therefore, in their present state, they can never become mature Christians, because the Scripture says:

> *By this it is evident who are the children of God, and who are the children of the devil: whoever does not practice righteousness is not of God, nor is the one who does not love his brother.*
>
> —1 John 3:10 ESV

Because the church is producing so many "tares," this problem has become an epidemic throughout the world. Did you know that people are actually going to hell because they refuse to become a Christian after what they've seen the phony Christians (tares) doing? Talk about satanic deception!

Sincerity Is Not the Key to Spiritual Well-Being

SINCERITY IS A KEY ASPECT of any religious belief. But we have a tendency to rely on our sincerity instead of the truth. You should never base your eternal destiny on the sincerity of your intellect or your heart. You must never allow that to occur because "sincerity" is a neutral characteristic. It works just as well for evil as it does for good. Think of the evil that is being done in this world today under the cloak of "sincere belief." Remember the Pharisees? They sincerely thought they were serving God when they crucified His Son (and of course, they were right—but not in the manner that was in their heart). Even though they were the religious leaders of their day, they were so caught up in their "traditions" that they didn't recognize the very Son of God when He walked among them.

What a tragedy! And if misdirected sincerity could happen to them, it can happen to the religious leaders of today—and it can happen to *you*! So please, don't rely on the sincerity of your heart and mind! Rely instead on the Word of God. The fully balanced Word of God. Don't make a Doctrine out of a singular verse as some do. That's why we have over 30,000 denominations in the world. Each one thinking they're the best.

If you sincerely believe you are a true Christian, but that fact is not backed up by *Great Commission fruit in your life*, then you are sincerely fooling yourself, and the results will be tragic for all eternity.

How Can I Tell If I Am a Mature Christian?

I HAVE DEVELOPED A SPIRITUAL checklist against which you can measure your life. When you use it to evaluate yourself, if there is any possibility that you are *not* a mature Christian, then please follow the suggestions at the end of this book—before it is too late.

Here Is the Checklist:

If you have been a Christian for two or more years, and you are still immature as a Christian, then you could still be a baby Christian, or chaff, because Scripture says:

Awake to righteousness, and sin not; for some have not the knowledge of God: I speak this to your shame.

—1 Corinthians 15:34

If you profess to be a Christian, but you're not doing anything to evangelize those in your sphere of influence, then you could still be a baby Christian, or a Tare, because scripture warns you:

> *Every tree that bringeth not forth good fruit is hewn down, and cast into the fire.*
>
> —Matthew 7:19

If you profess to be a Christian, but you lack an intimate relationship with the living Christ, then you could still be a baby Christian, or a Tare, because scripture says:

> *Not every one that saith unto me, Lord, Lord, shall enter into the kingdom of heaven; but he that doeth the will of my Father which is in heaven. Many will say to me in that day, Lord, Lord, have we not prophesied in thy name? and in thy name have cast out devils? and in thy name done many wonderful works? And then will I profess unto them, I never knew you: depart from me, ye that work iniquity.*
>
> —Matthew 7:21–23

If you profess to be a Christian, but you have become a lethargic Pew sitter who lacks the power of God in their life, then you could still be a baby Christian, or a Tare, because scripture says:

How Can I Tell If I Am a Mature Christian?

Having a form of godliness, but denying the power thereof: from such turn away.

—2 Timothy 3:5

If you profess to be a Christian, but you are just a "hearer of the word" and not a "doer of the word," then you could still be a baby Christian, or a Tare, because scripture says:

But it shall come to pass, if thou wilt not hearken unto the voice of the Lord thy God, to observe to do all his commandments and his statutes which I command thee this day; that all these curses shall come upon thee, and overtake thee.

—Deuteronomy 28:15

Jesus answered and said unto him, If a man love me, he will keep my words: and my Father will love him, and we will come unto him, and make our abode with him. He that loveth me not keepeth not my sayings: and the word which ye hear is not mine, but the Father's which sent me.

—John 14:23–24

But be ye doers of the word, and not hearers only, deceiving your own selves.

—James 1:22

There Is Only One Thing Worse Than Going to Hell

If you profess to be a Christian, but you never read the Bible or have faith in the word of God, then you could still be a baby Christian, or a Tare, because the scripture says:

And ye have not his word abiding in you: for whom he hath sent, him ye believe not. Search the scriptures; for in them ye think ye have eternal life: and they are they which testify of me. And ye will not come to me, that ye might have life.

—John 5:38–40

For unto us was the gospel preached, as well as unto them: but the word preached did not profit them, not being mixed with faith in them that heard it.

—Hebrews 4:2

If you profess to be a Christian, but you don't pray throughout the day, then you could still be a baby Christian, because Scripture says:

Watch and pray, that ye enter not into temptation: the spirit indeed is willing, but the flesh is weak.

—Matthew 26:41

How Can I Tell If I Am a Mature Christian?

Watch ye therefore, and pray always, that ye may be accounted worthy to escape all these things that shall come to pass, and to stand before the Son of man.

—LUKE 21:36

Pray without ceasing.

—1 THESSALONIANS 5:17

If you profess to be a Christian, but your life consists of nothing more than a shallow knowledge about Jesus Christ, combined with occasional religious activity after the traditions of your denomination, then you are probably a misguided Christian, because scripture says the following about the leadership some people sit under:

Making the word of God of none effect through your tradition, which ye have delivered: and many such like things do ye.

—MARK 7:13

If you sincerely believe that Jesus Christ is abiding in your life, but you are not doing anything to abide in Him, then you are probably not a Christian, because Scripture says:

*If a man abide **not** in me, he is cast forth as a branch, and is withered; and men gather them, and cast them into the fire, and they are burned.*

—JOHN 15:6

There Is Only One Thing Worse Than Going to Hell

If you profess to be a Christian, but you are in jail for something other than the cause of Christ, then you could still be a baby Christian, or a Tare, because scripture says:

Now the works of the flesh are manifest, which are these; adultery, fornication, uncleanness, lasciviousness, idolatry, witchcraft, hatred, variance, emulations, wrath, strife, seditions, heresies, envyings, murders, drunkenness, revellings, and such like: of the which I tell you before, as I have also told you in time past, that they which do such things shall not inherit the kingdom of God.

—Galatians 5:19–21

If you profess to be a Christian, but lying, habitually cheating on your taxes, and withholding financial giving are habits in your life, and you have no interest in changing, then you could still be a baby Christian, because Scripture says:

Wherefore putting away lying, speak every man truth with his neighbour: for we are members one of another.

—Ephesians 4:25

Let him that stole steal no more: but rather let him labour, working with his hands the thing which is good, that he may have to give to him that needeth.

—Ephesians 4:28

How Can I Tell If I Am a Mature Christian?

Will a man rob God? Yet ye have robbed me. But ye say, Wherein have we robbed thee? In tithes and offerings.

—Malachi 3:8

If you profess to be a Christian, but Christ and your spiritual leaders mean so little to you that you don't even bother to get to your fellowship or church meetings on time, then you could still be a baby Christian, because Scripture says:

Obey them that have the rule over you, and submit yourselves: for they watch for your souls, as they that must give account, that they may do it with joy, and not with grief: for that is unprofitable for you.

—Hebrews 13:17

If reading this study is offensive to you, or if it makes you angry, then you could still be a baby Christian, or a tare, because Scripture says:

For every one that doeth evil hateth the light, neither cometh to the light, lest his deeds should be reproved.

—John 3:20

If there is anything in your life that is more important than your relationship with Jesus Christ, such as sports, entertainment, your job, sleep, money, possessions, or another person, then you could still be a baby Christian, because Scripture says:

He that loveth father or mother more than me is not worthy of me: and he that loveth son or daughter more than me is not worthy of me. And he that taketh not his cross, and followeth after me, is not worthy of me. He that findeth his life shall lose it: and he that loseth his life for my sake shall find it.

—MATTHEW 10:37–39

Does this mean that every Christian who commits an occasional sin is not a Christian? No . . . absolutely not! But if you profess to be a Christian and you are still committing some form of habitual sin/s, then you are an immature Christian, and in danger of hellfire because Scripture says:

Now the works of the flesh are manifest, which are these; adultery, fornication, uncleanness, lasciviousness, idolatry, witchcraft, hatred, variance, emulations, wrath, strife, seditions, heresies, envyings, murders, drunkenness, revellings, and such like: of the which I tell you before, as I have also told you in time past, that they which do such things shall not inherit the kingdom of God.

—GALATIANS 5:19–21

Does this mean that every Christian who is immature is actually still a baby Christian? No . . . absolutely not! We progress from being a young child in the Lord, to becoming a young person in the Lord, and then finally we become mature in the Lord. Its called progressive sanctification, which is principally found in the twenty-one Epistles.

But if you profess to be a Christian and you are not consciously putting the world aside by applying the Word of God to your life, week by week, day by day, then you are still a baby Christian! Or maybe just a tare. (God forbid, for your sake).

> *For all that is in the world, the lust of the flesh, and the lust of the eyes, and the pride of life, is not of the Father, but is of the world.*
>
> —1 John 2:16

If you profess to be a Christian, but you watch movies that contain profanity, nudity, horror, and crime, or you tune in to soap operas that contain nothing but lasciviousness and sinful conduct, and you consider it entertaining, or you've become desensitized to any particular type of sin, then you could still be a baby Christian, because Scripture says:

> *For from within, out of the heart of men, proceed evil thoughts, adulteries, fornications, murders, thefts, covetousness, wickedness, deceit, lasciviousness, an evil eye, blasphemy, pride, foolishness: All these evil things come from within, and defile the man.*
>
> —Mark 7:21–23

But shun profane and vain babblings: for they will increase unto more ungodliness.

—2 Timothy 2:16

Garbage In = Garbage Out

If you profess to be a Christian, but you live as you choose, doing whatever you want, whenever you want, while sincerely believing that you are going to heaven, then you may not even be saved! You're probably just a tare, because a true Christian diligently develops a close and personal relationship with Jesus Christ. Not just about Him, but **with** Him.

If you profess to be a Christian, someone genuinely "saved from hell," but you have no real desire to let Jesus Christ be the Lord and Master of your life, then you're probably not a Christian, because Scripture says:

And why call ye me, Lord, Lord, and do not the things which I say?

—Luke 6:46

Remember ... Scripture is the only standard that we should use when trying to decide whether or not we are a true Christian.

Danger! Danger! Living your Christian life, always living in a spiritually immature manner, maybe for years and years, puts you in danger of not really being saved at the end of your life.

Why? Because if you're really saved, and not just religious, the Holy Spirit would have been guiding you into Christian maturity, as long as you were willing to obey and seek that level of maturity.

What does a true Christian look like?

But he that received seed into the good ground is he that heareth the word, and understandeth it; which also beareth fruit, and bringeth forth, some an hundredfold, some sixty, some thirty.

—MATTHEW 13:23

I believe that fruit is produced today by obeying the following Great Commission:

Go ye therefore, and teach all nations, baptizing them in the name of the Father, and of the Son, and of the Holy Ghost: [20] Teaching them to observe all things whatsoever I have commanded you: and, lo, I am with you alway, even unto the end of the world. Amen.

—MATTHEW 28:19,20

What Can I Do to Make Sure I Am Maturing in the Lord?

LIVE YOUR CHRISTIAN LIFE PROACTIVELY, not passively. On a daily basis, you need to exercise your will to be obedient unto the Lord.

You need to make sure you are not *professing* salvation without *possessing* it. For genuine salvation to occur, your life must be committed and given over to Jesus Christ. That means you have to "die to yourself" daily. Your attitude should be: *Not I, but Christ*. And this should be the case not once, but every day!

Your life needs to produce fruit. You can do this by making sure your works are ordered by the Lord. Anything else is just religiosity. The harvest is ready. The Holy Spirit is just waiting for someone to say, "Here am I, Lord, send me!"

You need to make sure that you are developing an intimate relationship with Jesus Christ. Just having knowledge *about*

Him is not enough. Daily obedience in applying the Word of God needs to be the progressive habit of your life.

You need to learn to hear the Lord's "still, small voice" so that He can properly guide you. You do this by abiding in the Lord and letting Him abide in you. Read the following verses found in the book of John:

> *I am the true vine, and my Father is the husbandman. Every branch in me that beareth not fruit he taketh away: and every branch that beareth fruit, he purgeth it, that it may bring forth more fruit. Now ye are clean through the word which I have spoken unto you. Abide in me, and I in you. As the branch cannot bear fruit of itself, except it abide in the vine; no more can ye, except ye abide in me. I am the vine, ye are the branches: He that abideth in me, and I in him, the same bringeth forth much fruit: for without me ye can do nothing. If a man abide not in me, he is cast forth as a branch, and is withered; and men gather them, and cast them into the fire, and they are burned. If ye abide in me, and my words abide in you, ye shall ask what ye will, and it shall be done unto you. Herein is my Father glorified, that ye bear much fruit; so shall ye be my disciples. As the Father hath loved me, so have I loved you: continue ye in my love. If ye keep my commandments, ye shall abide in my love; even as I have kept my Father's commandments, and abide in his love.*

What Can I Do to Make Sure I Am Maturing in the Lord?

These things have I spoken unto you, that my joy might remain in you, and that your joy might be full.

—John 15:1–11

In the preceding verses, the Lord outlines a few of the key things that need to occur in your life.

1. You need to abide in Jesus Christ and let Him abide in you (verses 4, 5, 7). *Abide* means you need to have faith in Him and yield to Him as your Lord and Master on a daily basis. Jesus "abides" in you by supporting you, guiding you, and loving you on a daily basis.

2. You need to obey Jesus Christ (verse 10).

3. You need to let Christ bear fruit through your life (verses 2, 8).

And now also the axe is laid unto the root of the trees: therefore every tree which bringeth not forth good fruit is hewn down, and cast into the fire.

—Matthew 3:10

But he that received seed into the good ground is he that heareth the word, and understandeth it; which also beareth fruit, and bringeth forth, some an hundredfold, some sixty, some thirty.

—Matthew 13:23

You also need to develop the character of Christ in your life, as indicated in the book of 2 Peter:

*And beside this, **giving all diligence**, add to your faith **virtue**; and to virtue **knowledge**; and to knowledge **temperance**; and to temperance **patience**; and to patience **godliness**; and to godliness **brotherly kindness**; and to brotherly kindness **charity**. For if these things be in you, and abound, they make you that ye shall neither be barren nor unfruitful in the knowledge of our Lord Jesus Christ. But he that lacketh these things is blind, and cannot see afar off, and hath forgotten that he was purged from his old sins. Wherefore the rather, brethren, give diligence to make your calling and election sure: for if ye do these things, ye shall never fall: for so an entrance shall be ministered unto you abundantly into the everlasting kingdom of our Lord and Saviour Jesus Christ.*

—2 Peter 1:5–11

Here Is Another Checklist to Follow

- ☐ Find a group of Christians with whom to fellowship.
- ☐ Set aside time to frequently meet with them.
- ☐ Focus on developing a deeper walk with Christ.
- ☐ Focus on the areas indicated within this study.
- ☐ Diligently apply those things that you are being taught.
- ☐ Make these activities a priority in your life.
- ☐ Go out and help someone else by mentoring them.
- ☐ Don't let the enemy cause you to be double-minded.

DOUBLE-MINDEDNESS OCCURS WHEN YOU constantly change your mind about doing something. Your thoughts are like the waves of the ocean, coming and going, in and out.

Your eternal destiny depends upon you having a close, intimate, obedient relationship with Jesus Christ! If all of the spiritual things indicated in this study are occurring in your life, then you can be assured that your profession of faith is sound. You don't have to worry about being an immature, underperforming, weak, spiritual piece of unproductive chaff, or a spiritually barren tare!

Benediction

Now unto him that is able to do exceeding abundantly above all that we ask or think, according to the power that worketh in us, unto him be glory in the church by Christ Jesus throughout all ages, world without end.

—Ephesians 3:20–21

God bless you and may your life be infused with the life of Jesus Christ, to His glory and your spiritual benefit! Amen.

Ch. Dr. Dave, your servant in the Lord

About the Author

I prefer not to ring my own bell, so to speak, because...

"He must increase, but I must decrease."

—John 3:30

However, there are those who require credentials if for no other reason than to give them satisfaction that the person speaking is sufficiently trained and experienced. Those who need credentials will appreciate that I am an honorably discharged military veteran, a born-again Christian for over sixty years, an ordained minister, and a mature Christian with a seminary education consisting of a B.Div., an M.Div., and a D.R.E.

I have held every position in the institutional church from a bus pastor to assistant pastor. I have been involved in every type of church, from house churches to megachurches. I am trained as a police chaplain, a general aviation chaplain, and a house church coach. I have written over thirty booklets, all on progressive sanctification.

The apostle Paul made tents for a living. Throughout my Christian life, the Lord has provided for me in similar fashion, because I am also credentialed and experienced in various secular occupations, both white collar and blue collar. My principal business activities outside of the ministry have included ventures in federal law enforcement, and regulatory enforcement, corporate security consulting, coaching in business profitability strategies, aviation journalism, and sales and marketing. I have had a very adventurous life, combining both spiritual and secular activities.

However, in the mixture, although I became an expert in religion, I was not an expert in a divine and deeply abiding relationship with Jesus Christ. Thank God that Jesus Christ is merciful and forgiving. It took two flat-line heart attacks to wake me up to the truth of my need for a greater evolution of progressive sanctification in my life.

The devil tried to kill me, but the Lord wasn't ready for me yet, so He brought me back from death twice! I'm living on borrowed time.

I had been satisfied living only by following the tenets of religious tradition. The devil tried to kill me before I could learn otherwise. After my health recovery, I knew for certain that more was required of me.

Now that I have my priorities sorted out, I have chosen to lay all aside to better focus on the Godhead (Father, Son, and Holy Spirit). Jesus Christ is my King, my Lord, the Savior of my soul, and the Provider of true "whole life" abundant living.

Allowing Him to live *through* you is what it really means to be "born again." We all know we should do so, but do we

About the Author

allow that to occur? It's so convenient to be religious, but I can testify that it's much more glorious to be *alive* in Christ.

To encapsulate the blessed and adventurous journey of my life, my personal testimony would have to be titled, "From the outhouse to the White House. Thank you, Lord.

Although I am trained in a variety of ministerial areas, I now principally focus on progressive sanctification combined with obedient application. That's the nucleus of my ministry because my spiritual gift is exhortation by example. That basically requires that we let the Holy Spirit minister *in* us and *through* us, instead of *from* us *to* Him. The Holy Spirit provides the guidance, the power, and the results; we provide the human obedience, love, and the footsteps in between. That way, only the Father, the Son, and the Holy Spirit get the glory, and Jesus gives us the reward.

I pray that I may be blessed as a servant of the Lord in helping you cultivate this same reality in your own life. And may you be blessed in receiving it as you read through my booklets.

So, there you are, folks. I pray that you'll be blessed by the mercies and grace of the Godhead for their sake and glory, and for your growth in righteousness. Amen.

CHAPLAIN DR. DAVE

www.ingramcontent.com/pod-product-compliance
Lightning Source LLC
Chambersburg PA
CBHW072137070526
44585CB00016B/1718